THE CHALLENGE FOR MEN

CHRISTIAN GROWTH IN SPIRITUAL LEADERSHIP: PERSONAL GROWTH JOURNAL

GLENN DAILY

CYPRESS

Copyright © 2025 by Glenn Daily

The Challenge for Men: Christian Growth in Spiritual Leadership

Catalog in Publication

Daily, Glenn
The challenge for men: Christian growth in spiritual leadership: facilitator's guide/
Glenn Daily
p. cm.

1. Christian leadership. 2. Men–Christian life I. Author. II. Title.
248.842 DDC21
ISBN: 978-1-956811-88-9 (pbk.) ; 978-1-956811-89-6 (ebook).

Cover designed by Glenn Daily and Brittany Vander Maas
For more information:

Cypress Publications
PO Box HCU
3625 Helton Drive
Florence, Alabama 35630

www.hcu.edu/publications

The Challenge

I took The Challenge

_____

Name

_____

Dates You Took The Challenge
Month/Day/Year through Month/Day/Year

_____

Name of Congregation

_____

City and State

Challenge 1

Characteristic _____

Challenge _____

1. State your name.

   _____

2. Give the name of your family members, and give a brief introduction of each member.

   _____
   _____
   _____

3. Provide your occupation and a brief work history.

_____

_____

_____

4. What was your hometown?

_____

_____

5. How long have you lived in this area of the country?

_____

_____

_____

6. How long have you been a member or visitor of this congregation?

_____

7. State the names of any relatives you have at this congregation.

_____

_____

_____

8. Where are you, and where do you want to be spiritually?

_____

_____

_____

_____

CHALLENGE 2

Characteristic _____

Challenge _____

1. State the passage of scripture.

_____

_____

_____

2. Introduce the scripture and context.

_____

_____

_____

_____

_____

_____

3. Which scripture did you read?

_____

_____

4. State how this scripture relates to your life.

_____

_____

_____

_____

_____

_____

5. Tell what the scripture means to you personally.

_____

_____

_____

_____

_____

_____

6. How have you or someone you know applied this scripture in life?

_____

_____

CHALLENGE 3

Characteristic _____

Challenge _____

1. Within the devotional:

- Have all members of your family (or invited friends) present
- State what God's word means to your life
- Introduce the scripture and context
- Read the scripture
- Comment on how this scripture relates to our lives
- Ask family members to give their thoughts on the scripture
- Close by leading a prayer.

2. Tell what passage of scripture you used and what the passage means to your life.

_____

_____

_____

_____

_____

_____

3. Which scripture did you read?

_____

_____

4. Who were the individuals present for the devotional?

_____

_____

_____

_____

5. How did the individuals present react to the devotional time together?

_____

_____

_____

_____

_____

6. What were some of their comments?

_____

_____

_____

_____

_____

_____

_____

_____

_____

7. Where and when can you present another devotional?

_____

_____

_____

_____

_____

CHALLENGE 4

Characteristic _____

Challenge _____

1. With whom did you visit?

_____
_____
_____

2. When did you visit the person(s)?

_____
_____
_____

3. Where did you visit?

_____

_____

_____

4. What did you learn about the person(s)?

_____

_____

_____

_____

_____

_____

5. How did the person(s) respond to your visit?

_____

_____

_____

_____

_____

_____

6. What was most uncomfortable to you about the visit?

_____

_____

_____

_____

_____

_____

7. How did completing the visit make you feel?

_____

_____

_____

_____

_____

_____

8. Will this visit encourage you in making more visits?

_____

_____

_____

_____

_____

_____

CHALLENGE 5

Characteristic _____

Challenge _____

1. With whom did you visit?

   _____
   _____
   _____

2. When did you visit?

   _____
   _____
   _____

3. Where did you visit?

_____

_____

_____

4. What did you learn about the leader?

_____

_____

_____

_____

_____

_____

_____

_____

5. Ask—How do you conform to the image of Christ? What answer did the leader give?

_____

_____

_____

_____

_____

_____

_____

_____

_____

_____

_____

6. Ask—How can I mature as a Christian? What answer did the leader give?

_____

_____

_____

_____

_____

_____

_____

_____

_____

_____

_____

_____

_____

_____

_____

_____

7. How did the couple respond to your visit?

_____

_____

_____

_____

_____

8. What was least comfortable about this visit? What apprehensions did you have?

_____

_____

_____

_____

_____

_____

9. What was most enjoyable about the visit?

_____

_____

_____

_____

_____

_____

10. What are your takeaways from this visit?

_____

_____

_____

_____

_____

_____

CHALLENGE 6

Characteristic _____

Challenge _____

1. When and where did the face-to-face meeting take place?

_____
_____
_____

2. What was the circumstance or situation that you referenced?

_____
_____
_____
_____
_____

_____

3. What was the person's initial reaction to the conversation?

_____
_____
_____
_____
_____
_____

4. How did the individual respond during the conversation?

_____
_____
_____
_____
_____
_____
_____
_____
_____

5. How did the individual end the conversation?

_____
_____
_____
_____
_____
_____
_____

_____

_____

6. Do you think forgiveness took place?

_____

_____

_____

_____

_____

_____

7. Do you believe the conversation helped your relationship?

_____

_____

_____

_____

_____

_____

8. How will this meeting help you in future situations?

_____

_____

_____

_____

_____

_____

_____

CHALLENGE 7

Characteristic _____

Challenge _____

1. Whom did you invite, or with whom did you have a conversation?

_____
_____
_____

2. When did you speak with the person?

_____
_____
_____

3. Where did you talk with the individual?

_____

_____

_____

4. Did you invite the individual to worship service and Bible study, or start a conversation on faith?

_____

_____

_____

5. Does the person have a religious background?

_____

_____

_____

_____

_____

_____

6. What was the individual's initial reaction to your request?

_____

_____

_____

7. What was the individual's response to the conversation?

_____

_____

_____

_____
_____
_____

8. Were you or the individual with whom you spoke the most uncomfortable and why?

_____
_____
_____
_____
_____
_____

9. What did you gain from the experience?

_____
_____
_____
_____
_____
_____

CHALLENGE 8

Characteristic _____

Challenge _____

1. When and where did you complete this challenge?

_____

_____

_____

2. How long did you study?

_____

_____

_____

_____

_____

_____

3. What passages of scripture or topics did you study?

_____
_____
_____
_____
_____
_____

4. On which specific scriptures did you meditate?

_____
_____
_____
_____
_____
_____

5. For what did you pray?

_____
_____
_____
_____
_____
_____

6. How did you feel during this challenge?

_____

_____

_____

_____

_____

_____

7. How is your current prayer life?

_____

_____

_____

_____

_____

_____

_____

_____

8. What is your current frequency of studying God's word?

_____

_____

_____

_____

_____

9. What did a day of study and prayer do for you?

_____

_____

_____

_____

_____

_____

_____

_____

_____

10. How did this challenge experience change or reinforce your future behavior?

_____

_____

_____

_____

_____

_____

_____

_____

_____

CHALLENGE 9

Characteristic _____

Challenge _____

1. What is the Christian leadership attribute?

_____
_____
_____
_____
_____
_____

2. How may the characteristic be applied in Christian living?

_____
_____

_____

_____

_____

_____

3. How have you or someone you know applied the attribute?

_____

_____

_____

_____

_____

_____

_____

_____

_____

4. How did you feel in preparing the speech?

_____

_____

_____

_____

_____

5. What was the most difficult part of this challenge for you?

_____

_____

_____

_____

_____
_____
_____
_____
_____

6. What did you like best about this challenge?

_____
_____
_____
_____
_____
_____
_____

7. How will you build on this experience?

_____
_____
_____
_____
_____
_____
_____
_____

CHALLENGE 10

Characteristic _____

Challenge _____

Possible themes or comments that your speech may include:

- What I gained from The Challenge experience
- How I may apply what I learned or experienced in The Challenge
- How I increased my leadership skills or grew spiritually
- My most difficult challenge and why
- The challenge I enjoyed the most and why
- The most surprising incident in The Challenge
- Where I go from here in my Christian leadership development

1. Notes in preparing your speech follow:

_____

_____

_____

_____

_____

_____

_____

_____

_____

_____

_____

2. What themes or subjects did your speech contain?

_____

_____

_____

_____

_____

_____

_____

_____

3. What did you gain from The Challenge experience?

_____

_____

_____
_____
_____
_____
_____
_____
_____
_____
_____
_____

4. How can you apply what you learned or experienced in The Challenge?

_____
_____
_____
_____
_____
_____
_____
_____
_____

5. How did you increase your leadership skills and grow spiritually during The Challenge?

_____
_____
_____
_____

_____

_____

_____

_____

6. What was the most difficult challenge and why?

_____

_____

_____

_____

_____

_____

_____

_____

_____

_____

_____

7. Which challenge did you enjoy the most, and why did you enjoy this challenge?

_____

_____

_____

_____

_____

_____

_____

_____

_____

8. What was the most surprising incident in The Challenge and why was this incident the most surprising?

_____

_____

_____

_____

_____

_____

_____

_____

_____

9. Where will I go from here in my Christian leadership development?

_____

_____

_____

_____

_____

_____

_____

_____

10. My speech—page 1.

_____

_____

_____

Wild Transformation

by Matthew Morine

CYPRESS

To see the full catalog of Heritage Christian University Press and
its imprint, Cypress Publications, visit
www.hcupress.edu